Wild About
Babies

Jack Hanna

Rick Prebeg

H
HARVEST HOUSE PUBLISHERS
EUGENE, OREGON

Special Thanks

Thanks to the Columbus Zoo staff, volunteers, and Zoo board—especially Sally South, Don Winstel, Dan Hunt, Dusty Lombardi, Doug Warmolts, Harry Peachey, and Kate Noice—for their valuable contributions to *Wild About Babies* (and for keeping the animals at the zoo happy and healthy!). Thanks also to Kimberly Sullivan for helping to make this project possible. And a thank you to the animals of the world for being such a great inspiration to us all.

JACK AND RICK

Text copyright © 2004 by Jack Hanna and Rick Prebeg

Published by Harvest House Publishers
Eugene, Oregon 97402
www.harvesthousepublishers.com

Library of Congress Cataloging-in-Publication Data

Hanna, Jack, 1947-
    Wild about babies / Jack Hanna, Rick Prebeg.
        p. cm.
    ISBN 0-7369-1208-8
    1. Parenting--Religious aspects--Christianity. 2.
Animals—Infancy—Miscellanea. I. Prebeg, Rick A. II. Title.
    BV4529.H33 2004
    242' .645—dc22

              2003015291

For other exciting Jack Hanna products or information on licensing, please contact his licensing agent at ZStrategies@aol.com.

All artwork appearing in this book is licensed through Mill Pond Licensing, Venice, Florida, and may not be reproduced without permission.

Artwork © Carl Brenders: "On a Journey," p. 1; "Rocky Camp—Cougar Family," p. 2; "Just Shy of Sly," p. 21; "Mother of Pearls," front cover and p. 26; "Polar Bear Cub," p. 29; "A Threatened Symbol," p. 32; "Close to Mom," p. 41; "Tall Grass Tiger," p. 45.

Artwork © Rod Frederick: "The High and the Mighty," p. 6; "Earning His Stripes," p. 34.

Artwork © Terry Isaac: "Refuge," p. 14; "The Lesson—Bobcats," p. 21; "Father's Day," p. 25; "Out of the Storm," p. 30; "Koala," p. 48.

Artwork © John Seerey-Lester: "Dry Season—African Elephants," p. 5; "Panda Trilogy—Mom and Baby," p. 10; "Panda Trilogy—Panda in Tree," p. 12; "Celebrating Hua Mei," p. 13; "Mountain Cradle," p. 16; "The Thinker," p. 16; "High and Mighty—Gorilla," p. 17; "Togetherness—Lioness with Cub," p. 22; "Amboseli Child—African Elephant," p. 36; "Child of the Outback," p. 48.

Artwork © Daniel Smith: "Samburu Crossing—Elephants," p. 20; "Family Pride," p. 24; "Black Rhinos," p. 38; "Tiger in Water," p. 42; "Koala," p. 46.

Design and production by Koechel Peterson & Associates, Inc., Minneapolis, Minnesota

Harvest House Publishers has made every effort to trace the ownership of all poems and quotes. In the event of a question arising from the use of a poem or quote, we regret any error made and will be pleased to make the necessary correction in future editions of this book.

04 05 06 07 08 09 10 11 12 13 / NG / 10 9 8 7 6 5 4 3 2

CONTENTS

The Amazing World of Wild Animals

The Amazing World of Wild Animals

Babies are such sweet beginnings.

I'm wild about babies, but then, I think everyone is, don't you? Human babies are adorable, loving, and completely dependent upon us. Their tiny forms and sheer newness make babies so endearing. These same characteristics draw us to baby animals—if you've ever visited a zoo, you know that baby animals are always the number one attraction.

I think we would all agree that baby animals are really, really cute. Lion and tiger cubs are little fluff balls, just like kittens at home (except a little more ferocious); guinea pigs are born with their eyes open and with hair, looking just like miniature adults; baby giraffes are wondrous, long-legged, skinny creatures whose first steps mimic a man on stilts; grizzly cubs look just like lovable teddy bears.

Over the years I've been fortunate to observe many wild animals and their babies, both at the zoo and in their natural environment. You know, sometimes I think animals have life down pat. After all, they've been around for quite a while, so they've had a lot of practice. You don't have to watch for long to begin seeing that humans can learn some valuable lessons from the animal kingdom. For example, the family unit of lions (the "pride") is integral to the cubs' survival in the wild, and the extended families within monkey troops play a large part in the development of baby monkeys. Throughout the amazing animal kingdom, parents demonstrate admirable qualities when rearing their young—qualities of patience, tolerance, gentleness, and perseverance. However, they don't display the anger, disappointment, and envy that often interfere with the family social unit.

While writing this book, I remembered a fascinating story from the wilds of Africa. It didn't quite fit into any chapter of its own, but it's worth repeating and sharing.

Lions are fierce predators, and the females work cooperatively during their hunts. Most of the lion's prey is medium-to-large antelope and zebra. When hunger strikes and a lion spots an antelope, all systems are "go" for a hunt.

Well, a lioness at the Samburu Game Reserve in Kenya, Africa, was recently observed in an unprecedented series of events involving a little baby oryx. An oryx is a type of antelope—and yes, also a type of lion food.

This intriguing lioness came across a herd of oryx and, strangely enough, didn't begin to hunt. Instead—and in a most un-lionlike fashion—she purposely separated a newborn oryx calf from its group and began caring for it as if it were her own. During the next few weeks, the lioness was seen roaming the wilds with the tottering oryx baby alongside. She spent her days protecting the little one, chasing away other predators. Rangers in the Samburu area watched this incredible twosome and aptly named the lioness "Kamuniak" (Blessed One). Even more surprising, Kamuniak would actually let the baby oryx return to the herd so that it could nurse from its mother. Once the baby was full, though, this amazing lioness would again claim "her" baby.

One night weeks later, the mother oryx miraculously wandered into the lioness's area and saw her baby. Mother and baby met and left to rejoin the herd—this time for good. Sadly, reports say that in the following days the lioness was seen frantically searching for her "lost baby."

This lioness quickly became famous after adopting six different baby oryx—animals that would have normally been her prey. Seeing Kamuniak with the baby oryx is reminiscent of the utopian scene of the lion lying with the lamb. I've never before seen or heard anything like this in the world of wild animals.

The animal kingdom is diverse and intriguing. Single parents, extended families, and committed couples work hard to raise their offspring so that they may crawl, swing, and fly away to independent lives of their own. You most likely play an important role in the life of a child. Humans can be both entertained and inspired by the passion animal parents have for their young. I invite you to sit back and enjoy some of the amazing creatures that share the world with us.

*We made a wish
and you came true!*
AUTHOR UNKNOWN

Someone to Watch Over Me
Giraffes

I was about to witness an amazing event. A giraffe at the Columbus Zoo was ready to give birth, and I'd never seen anything like this before. Some animals—such as the giraffe, antelope, camel, and elephant— give birth while standing up. This may be what's normal for the mother, but for the newborn giraffe, seeing the world for the first time as his head pops out, it must appear to be an awfully long way to the ground.

Some babies seem to be born almost instantly, but giraffes take a while. We were all anxiously watching as the tall mother giraffe walked around her enclosure just before the impending birth. Suddenly, we noticed two tiny hooves below her tail, but nothing more happened right away. More time passed, and then the baby giraffe's head emerged! We waited another 45 minutes before the baby was born, falling five to six feet to the ground with a big splash.

Before you were conceived I wanted you
Before you were born I loved you
Before you were here an hour I would die for you
This is the miracle of life.

MAUREEN HAWKINS

Though the baby seemed a bit stunned, this process is perfectly normal (it happens exactly the same way on the golden savannas of the African veldt). Our giraffe was a model mother. Just after her baby dropped beneath her, she hovered over it on her long, stiltlike legs, protecting the newborn. If a predator were to approach, the mother giraffe would kick straight out with her formidable front legs!

After just a short time, the mother began nudging the little one, trying to get him to stand up on his own. What a sight! I think the term "awkward" was invented for giraffe babies. He tried to extend one foreleg, then the other—and suddenly he fell backward! The little giraffe tried again and again until, finally, he raised his spindly body off the ground. The look on his face was "Now, what do I do?" Well, the mother quickly answered that by standing over her baby so that he could enjoy his first, and most essential, drink of milk. In nature it is imperative that a baby giraffe gets on its feet (sorry—hooves) quickly so that it can run with all the others.

Out in the wild, during the first week or so, a calf will actually lie out half the day and most of the night, carefully guarded by his mother. Mamma giraffe usually stays within 11 to 25 yards of her offspring, although mothers may stray over 100 yards from a hidden calf and even leave it alone to go to water. The increased security of a maternity group guarding calves in a crèche allows individual mothers to go farther and stay away longer. However, calves are rarely left totally unattended, and absent mothers usually return before dark to suckle their offspring and stay with them overnight.

We need to find God,
and He cannot be found
in noise and restlessness.
God is the friend of silence.
See how nature—
trees, flowers, grass—
grows in silence; see the stars,
the moon and the sun,
how they move in silence...
We need silence to be
able to touch souls.

MOTHER TERESA

Lessons from the Wild

Giraffes are majestic creatures. When they gallop across the grasslands, they seem to glide. They

tower above all other animals and have a fantastic view of their world. My impression of these

magnificent animals is that they don't often seem upset or angry. They just take their time,

rarely make a sound, eat only the choicest of acacias, don't bother other animals, and just glide

along through life. These are lessons I love noticing in the wild.

A mother's arms are made
of tenderness, and children
sleep soundly in them.

VICTOR HUGO

Mother Bear
Giant Pandas

I was far, far away from home...and I was very aware of it. Sometimes when I travel around the world, the places I end up in don't feel that different, but this time was an exception. Although I don't speak a lot of languages, I usually know how to express a few common phrases and try to fit in—but not here. About the only word I could even hope to pronounce was "hello." The people were very friendly and hospitable, but their customs were unfamiliar— for example, I noticed that when they ate bananas, they peeled them from the bottom instead of the top. Most people started their days by riding bicycles or walking to work. They shopped at open markets for fresh fish, vegetables, and meat in large, ultra-modern cities with traffic jams and skyscrapers. I was in China.

I was here with a delegation from the Columbus Zoo. We were being hosted by the Chinese government because we were discussing an animal exchange. We were offering two African cheetahs (rarely seen in China's zoos) for two giant pandas.

The giant panda may look like a lovable teddy bear, but it can be as dangerous as any large predator. Black and white, this animal lives a solitary life and munches bamboo high in China's misty mountain forests. Because there are only about 1000 giant pandas living in the wild, they are classified as an endangered species. Efforts to breed pandas in special animal reserves have not been highly successful when compared to other species, and the only way to save this magnificent animal from extinction is to preserve its homeland. Unfortunately, much of the panda's natural habitat is being destroyed by humans.

Our Chinese hosts told me they had a special surprise for me when we visited the zoo. We walked toward the panda exhibit, and I couldn't believe my eyes. There they were, giant pandas! No wonder everyone loves them—they are really adorable. One was sitting upright, clutching a piece of bamboo with its paw. Another one lumbered across the exhibit to relax in the shade. Next door was another panda area, and sitting under a tree limb was a young panda, probably only a few years old. Our friendly hosts invited us in, and with the help of zookeepers, I met the little black-and-white ball of fur. They even encouraged me to pet it (something I normally wouldn't have done), so I knelt down, reached out, and touched. It was just as fascinating as you can imagine.

I was really impressed by that experience, and I wanted others to be able to see pandas firsthand here in the United States. In the end, our Chinese hosts agreed to the animal

exchange. Several years later, two wonderful giant pandas— along with their zookeepers—journeyed across the ocean to visit the Columbus Zoo for a summer. It was really a great feeling to know that the people of Ohio and vicinity could see pandas in person—just as I did in China.

A mother is the truest friend we have, when trials, heavy and sudden,

fall upon us, when adversity takes the place of prosperity,

when friends who rejoice with us in our sunshine,

desert us when troubles thicken around us, still will she cling to us,

and endeavor by her kind precepts and counsels to dissipate the clouds

of darkness, and cause peace to return to our hearts.

WASHINGTON IRVING

Lessons from the Wild

As in the case of a human child, a baby panda is helpless at birth and the mother must

attend to its every need. The cub weighs only three to five ounces and is hairless, blind,

and not highly mobile. The mother panda really has her paws full when she's rearing

a baby. Though the father panda has moved on and she's a single mother, the mother

panda manages to care for the little one while trying to forage for food to keep both

of them strong. That can be a big chore, because pandas digest only about one-fifth

of what they eat (in fact, to get enough nutrition from bamboo, a panda has to eat 15

percent of her body weight in 12 hours). Although the baby grows quickly, it will nurse

for about nine months and stay with the mother for almost three years.

Mother panda has no help at all—unlike in monkey societies, where aunts and older

siblings take part in rearing the baby. Yet she does not shy from her task in raising her

baby to eventually take its own place in the bamboo forests of China.

Model Behavior
Gorillas

Gorillas are probably the most intriguing animals I've met because we, as humans, have so much in common with them. When you are around gorillas for a while, it is difficult to see them as "animals." One look into a gorilla's eyes and you instantly realize there is a lot going on inside their minds. I've noticed this with the gorillas at the Columbus Zoo as well as the wild gorillas in Africa (Rwanda's Park des Volcans and Uganda's Impenetrable Forest).

Your children will become what you are;
so be what you want them to be.
DAVID BLY

The Columbus Zoo has a distinctive pedigree when it comes to its gorilla family. In 1956, Colo was the first gorilla in the world to be born into captivity. Things at the zoo must have agreed with her and her gorilla friends because, over the years, the family grew and grew. Colo is now a great-grandmother.

Gorillas are an endangered species. Because they reproduce very slowly, every gorilla birth is a special event. So special are gorilla babies that the moms are treated just like expectant humans. I have a good friend, a gynecologist for humans, who cares for our gorilla mothers as he would care for human moms—providing them with frequent examinations and ultrasounds. When Bridgette became pregnant, he did an ultrasound to see how things were looking and, to our surprise, we saw two tiny heads! Twinning in gorillas is almost unheard of. It has only been documented once before in a zoo, and the babies didn't live long. So we were all concerned about what would happen.

Because we wanted to minimize any distractions during this important birth, we set up cameras around Bridgette and watched via remote video from another building. One night about 11:00, my wife, Suzi, was looking at the TV monitor when suddenly, after weeks of volunteers watching around the clock, she noticed that Bridgette was "ready." At the time, probably more than a dozen zoo staff and volunteers huddled around the small TV screen. Bridgett calmly sat on her nest of hay, looked around, and then got up. Lying in the straw was her baby! She immediately became the perfect gorilla mother and picked up the baby, holding him close. She sat down again—undoubtedly very proud of her accomplishment—but something was different. She shifted her weight and stood up again—only to see another infant gorilla! This baby was still covered by the placenta, and Bridgette didn't seem to know what to do next.

Lessons from the Wild

A gorilla is similar to a human in that it experiences "childhood," a time that allows it to learn important gorilla etiquette and proper parenting skills from its parents and extended family members. This is the most important time of a young gorilla's life—much as it is with our kids—because these are the years that they observe, remember, and define a good parent. I'm reminded of Proverbs 22:6, "Train up a child in the way he should go and when he is old, he will not depart from it." It occurs to me that not only would this proverb apply to active teaching and training but passive modeling of good parenting as well.

As parents, we need to be aware of our "silent witness." We have the wonderful privilege of shaping a life that will touch the future.

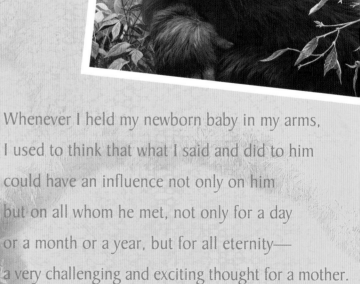

Whenever I held my newborn baby in my arms,
I used to think that what I said and did to him
could have an influence not only on him
but on all whom he met, not only for a day
or a month or a year, but for all eternity—
a very challenging and exciting thought for a mother.

ROSE KENNEDY

Normally, from the moment a gorilla baby enters the world, the mother immediately picks it up, breaks open the placenta and other surrounding membranes in order to let the baby breathe, and then holds her baby close so that nursing can begin.

She'll carry the little infant constantly, even when she is eating. Interestingly, good gorilla parenting is a learned behavior. Mother gorillas who haven't watched other gorillas care for youngsters often don't have adequate parental skills, and their babies often suffer or die prematurely. This usually isn't a problem in the wild (gorillas live in family groups that offer many learning experiences) but has been with animals in captivity years ago.

I realized this was Bridgette's situation. Because twinning is so rare with gorillas, Bridgette never had the opportunity to observe or learn what to do in the event that two babies were born instead of one. With one baby in tow and the other still lying on the ground, Bridgette began walking around her enclosure apparently anxious and confused. The staff and I knew that time was of the essence, and we would have to intervene in order to save the second baby.

The zookeepers called Bridgette into an open area adjacent to the baby and then shut the door behind her. Now, it was safe for the zoo staff to rush into the birthing area and remove the placental sac from the second baby. Luckily the baby was breathing! Bridgette never learned how to properly care for her twins, and there were no other gorillas there to show her how or help her. In the wild, not only does the female care for her baby, but the dominant male silverback—the leader of the gorilla troop— also lends a hand. And he defends the group ferociously! But ferocious as he may be, he'll let a youngster pounce on his belly while he's resting and pull his hair without reacting. In light of these "natural" limitations at the zoo, we decided it would have been unfair to force Bridgette to choose one baby over the other for her to rear. For the good of both little babies, the staff cared for them in the nursery. Today, some 20 years later, the twins have grown up, gorilla-style, and are big, big boys!

A Chimp off the Old Block
Chimpanzees

I was climbing deep into a jungle gorge in Uganda, Africa. The foliage was wet and the ground was soft with dead leaves. My film crew and I were searching for some creatures that lived in this amazing habitat. The gorge was divided by a river and filled with lush vegetation and was surrounded by a vast brown grassland, a very unusual situation indeed. From the air, Chambura Gorge looked like a sparkling emerald in the rough.

Well, the animals we were in search of saw—or heard—us as we were on our way. We couldn't see them, but the sudden ear-piercing vocalizations were unmistakable—CHIMPS! I had never before seen wild chimpanzees, and although I had had the privilege of raising one, these were really quite different. High, high in the trees they were, peering down at us. They were engaged in typical chimpanzee behavior—the kind displayed when intruders visit. Hooting and hollering, they even threw branches down at us. What a welcome! This was just the beginning of a journey that took us deep into the complex social lives of these special primates.

Chimpanzee babies, like humans, experience an "extended childhood" that is paramount to the infant's social, psychological, and physical development. Having extra time to be a kid means you can play more. Play behavior is very important to all young mammals, and especially so to the higher primates (chimps, bonobos, gorillas, and orangutans).

Growing up slowly allows chimp youngsters more time to learn (don't we all wish we could go back to our childhood days, only this time not rushing through them?). Learning is really important for primates, as it is with humans. Chimps must learn how to develop into proper chimp society members—what hand signals and vocalizations to use for communications, how to treat elder chimps versus same-age chimps, how to use body language, and of course, what types of food to eat. Interestingly, they learn by observing group members and then imitating and practicing what they've seen. Chimps have very few innate behaviors (also called instincts), so learning is critical. Socially deprived chimps do not develop normally.

Chimps travel in small family groups (consisting of a mother with dependent little ones) that are part of a much larger, loosely knit society. The family cares for each other and forages together. Figs are a favored snack, and when fig trees bear fruit, the whole group comes together, which is quite fun for all! I am reminded of when I was growing up as a boy and the great times we had at family gatherings.

When most animals look at their reflection, they think that they are looking at another creature. Not with us, of course. We see the person looking back at us and have instant recognition. The same is true with chimpanzees. A researcher once placed a dab of paint on a chimp's forehead and had him look into a mirror—the chimp looked at the image and raised his arm to touch the foreign substance on his forehead. Other animals may have reached out to the mirror, but not the chimp. These are highly intelligent forms of life (when you know a chimp, it's sometimes difficult referring to them as animals), and they are very deserving of our attention.

Like most everyone, I've always been fascinated with chimps. We see them on TV, in ads, and in circuses, marveling at how similar they are to us. But today we have a much different view of these "animals." The general feeling now is that having chimps dress up like people and ride bicycles and do other tricks is beneath them. Jane Goodall, the famous chimpanzee researcher, has studied chimps for more than 30 years in the wild. Through much of her work, we've come to know and respect them as very intelligent, highly social animals that care deeply about relationships. They suffer greatly from social isolation, much like a human would. Their world is highly complex, and we can learn many good things from observing it.

Lessons from the Wild

Human youngsters, like chimps, are learners. They are little sponges, soaking up every piece of informational moisture they come across. Have fun teaching them everything you can. They'll thank you for it in the future.

In the chimp community, older siblings (including males) often adopt their orphaned brothers or sisters. This is another sweet lesson we can learn. Good relationships with family members last a lifetime! If you and your extended family live near each other, encourage contact from aunts, uncles, and cousins. I love the adage "it takes a village to rear a child."

What families have in common the world around is that they are the place where people learn who they are and how to be that way.

HEAN ILLSLEY CLARKE

Most of all the other beautiful things
in life come by twos and threes,
by dozens and hundreds.
Plenty of roses, stars, sunsets,
rainbows, brothers, and sisters,
aunts and cousins, but only one
mother in the whole world.
KATE DOUGLAS WIGGIN

Family Pride
Lions

Sometimes working with wild animals can be a little dangerous. I'll never forget the day when one of my, say, "anxious" moments on safari involved a lovely pride of lions…

We were on location in Botswana, Africa, filming for my show *Animal Adventures*. One evening we watched as a pride of lions caught a wildebeest (lions hunt mostly at night). By the way, the wildebeest is one of the lion's favorite meals, and it is also one of the oddest-looking animals around. Wildebeest babies, called calves, are even more homely— bringing to mind the phrase "a face only a mother could love."

That night, the females from the pride got together and began searching for a meal. One of the lionesses spotted a small group of wildebeest. Immediately she crouched down in the high grass…the other lionesses fanned out and hid. When the moment was right, the lioness rushed the wildebeest while her helpers created confusion on the flanks, and in less than two minutes the lions had themselves a meal.

When you look at your life, the greatest happinesses are family happinesses.
DR. JOYCE BROTHERS

To maintain a joyful family requires much from both the parents and the children. Each member of the family has to become, in a special way, the servant of the others.

POPE JOHN PAUL II

23

Lessons from the Wild

The group dynamics of lions offer us a couple of important things to think about. When we are closely connected to a group, we can feel secure in the knowledge that we have a strong and committed support system, such as our family or church community, backing us up. Lions also show us that the health and success of the extended "family" depends on each member contributing to the well-being of the entire group. Lions stick together! In addition, lions respect and maintain order. That's not to say the male is more important then the female, for without female lions, male lions would have to hunt on their own. However, it is interesting to me that even in the wild, there is a natural order to things.

Let your children know that they can count on you to be there for them through the thick and thin. Honoring your spouse and children and respecting the order you and your partner have established for your family will give your wild babies a great sense of security and family pride.

Of course, they all shared—but not in the way you'd think. The leader of the pride, a powerful adult male lion (with a spectacular mane, I might add) heard the commotion and arrived at the scene. The lionesses reluctantly deferred to the male's hunger, and he ate his fill. Once his appetite was satiated, the lady lions moved in for their share. They pretty much cleaned the carcass, and then the cubs moved in hoping for a few last morsels.

Early the next morning we came upon our friends again—about 23 lions in all. Observing them, I couldn't help thinking about how a group of lions is a model of efficiency. Not only is cooperation key; so is the idea of a hierarchy. The way lions relate to one another ensures the survival of the pride as a whole. Now they were all busy relaxing after their meal from the night before and fun to watch.

The huge dominant male, leader of the pride, was just "lion" around. Playful cubs jumped on top of him, pulled his tail, and generally made pests of themselves. He didn't seem to mind. The smallest of cubs nursed from their mothers. Older cubs "fought" together—play-fighting is a very important means for young mammals to learn how to attack prey. So is watching their elders.

Remember when I started this story and said I had been a little…scared? When we had finished filming, our driver started the Land Rover. Instead of moving forward, we heard the distressing sound of spinning tires! We had sat for hours watching the lions, not realizing that our vehicle was resting in soft mud. The lions suddenly sensed that we were trying to get away but couldn't (a sign of weakness), and they perked up. We thought perhaps we were being eyed as dessert! Our driver made a radio call and asked for another Land Rover to pick us up. Once it arrived and pulled up next to us, we had to carefully climb out of our Rover and into the other—without stepping on the ground! Lions don't mind visitors as long as they stay seated, but if they stand up—or worse, get out—things can get dicey. Fortunately, we made our getaway safely.

Who ran to help me when I fell,
Or kissed the place to make it well?
My mother.
ANN TAYLOR

Cold Hands, Warm Heart

Polar Bears

    I clearly remember the first time I came eye to eye with a polar bear. It was at the Columbus Zoo when I first arrived as its director in 1978. I was making my rounds with the zookeepers to meet all the animals. Passing the polar bear display on the way to the interior, off-exhibit quarters, I was truly amazed with the great size of these animals, the largest of all land carnivores. A male can tip the scales at 1500 pounds and be 10 feet in length.

    After learning that Zero, one of our female bears, was pregnant, the animal-care staff decided to put a video surveillance camera on her. A polar bear birth is an exciting event, and everyone wanted to ensure that mother and baby were fine because the mother was inside a dark, isolated den. Mother and baby wouldn't emerge from the den for a few months.

Carl Brenders

> I will hug him, so that not any
> storm can come to him.
>
> JULIAN HAWTHORNE

Lessons from the Wild

It's amazing to witness how these naturally fierce adult bears allow themselves to be so quickly transformed into protective but tender, loving, gentle giants in the presence of their cubs. After spending time with the polar bears, I often think about how as parents, it's sometimes necessary and natural for us to assume the role of an aggressive, fierce hunter just to make a living and to survive the daily trials and tribulations of traffic jams, project deadlines, personality clashes, car repairs, and so on. Sometimes getting home safely and sanely is a victory unto itself.

Like the polar bear, we need to learn to leave that aggressive hunter at the door when we enter into the presence of our children. We need to allow ourselves to be transformed into the loving, attentive parents we were created to be by reminding ourselves of just how physically and emotionally fragile our children are. Once we realize how much our children depend upon us for their safety, we become more aware of the dangers that surround them and are more prepared to spring into action to protect them from harm.

Our own little cubs deserve our utmost love and tender care. Wrap your giant paw lovingly around your little cubs today and give 'em a great big bear hug!

Watching the videotape of the birth is something that I'll always remember. The first view was that of the mother bear lying on her back with the baby, aptly named Subzero, on top of her.

The baby was a mere fluff ball. She was only about 16 ounces and eight to ten inches in length and very frail-looking. Zero must have decided it was time for the little cub to nurse, for she moved the tiny one into position. Her massive paw (designed for killing) ever so gently cradled the newborn and positioned it for that important first taste of mother's milk—just amazing.

You see, the polar bear is well known as perhaps the most ferocious hunter in the animal world, and to see this gentle, caring side of this incredible creature was an eye-opener.

One morning in February, when the cub was a few months old, Zero decided it was time to bring her out of the den. The mother paused at the entrance of the display, looked around, and sniffed the cold, wintry air. She had her baby safely under her, between her legs. Walking around the display, she constantly had the baby in check—until one moment when the cub disappeared!

Zero was standing on the edge of the exhibit with a pool behind her. Being winter, the pool had been drained and the bottom was filled with hay bales. Well, Subzero, who was between her mother's legs, took a step back, and fell into the pool. It happened so fast that all I saw was that cute little head and two paws flying backward! Zero immediately sprang into action—polar bear parents are notorious for defending their young, even if it means death or harm to themselves. Zero stood on the edge of the pool making loud "snuffing" sounds toward Subzero. Balancing herself perfectly, Zero reached deep into the pool and grabbed the baby cub gently in her huge jaws and pulled her to safety.

A bundle of love to call your own has come into your hearts and home.
AUTHOR UNKNOWN

Helping Dreams Take Flight
Eagles

George and Georgina were longtime favorites of zoo visitors. Tremendous birds and our symbol of freedom, these bald eagles enjoyed a spacious flight enclosure complete with trees, fallen logs, a brook, and lots of vegetation.

Bald eagles pair for life. Maybe this commitment to each other was what made this exhibit such a popular attraction year after year. In November of one year, I watched as George and Georgina worked together to build their nest. I don't know if you've ever seen an eagle nest, but they are really large. Eagles usually use the same nest every year and add fresh material. Eventually, the nest can weigh as much as one ton.

A mother is someone
who dreams great dreams for you,
but then she lets you chase
the dreams you have for yourself
and loves you just the same.
AUTHOR UNKNOWN

We knew that sometime the following February an egg or two would be laid. Bald eagles are rare birds, and we wanted to ensure a successful hatching and fledging. To do so, we needed to monitor the process while minimizing our contact with the family. As with other births, we installed a video camera near the nest before the eagle chicks, or eaglets, were born. We also stopped vehicular traffic around the exhibit to reduce the amount of noise and pollution around the expectant family.

Early one cold winter morning, we saw Georgina staying put on the nest and knew she must have laid eggs. In fact, she was incubating two of them! We fed the eagles daily by laying out food for them, but Georgina wasn't about to leave her nest to feed herself. Instead, George retrieved the food and brought it to her so she could perform her primary responsibility at the time, which was keep the eggs insulated and at a relatively constant temperature. Later on in the incubation period, George and Georgina took turns keeping the nest warm and protected.

Thirty-one days later, both eggs hatched, and two adorable eaglets emerged out of their shells and into the loving nest their proud parents had prepared. All we could see of them were their fluffy little gray heads peeking out of the nest when Georgina decided to take a break. Since we could now get a look at them, it was time for names…Freedom and Liberty.

Terry Cloose

The zoo is involved in an important breeding program for bald eagles with an aim to increase the wild eagle population. These two young eagles were about to see what living in the wild was all about. In April, after they had a little time to learn from their parents and grow in size and stature, we carefully removed them from the security of their parents' nest and transported them to a perfect eagle habitat in a wilderness area in Tennessee. The two growing eagles were treated like kings as they were flown to Tennessee and then driven into the forest to their "hacking tower." A hacking tower is a wooden box "nest" with one side open to the forest with bars to keep the birds inside. This hacking tower would afford the young eagles protection from the elements while they received the opportunity to experience their natural habitat—the sights, sounds, and scents of the forest as well as other wildlife, including eagles.

For eight weeks, biologists sent food to the eagles every day by way of a conveyer system. These two eagles from Columbus were living the good life.

Then the exciting day arrived. It was time to release these beautiful birds into the wild, and we hoped that their parents, together with the team from the zoo, had adequately prepared them to adapt to their new environment and to fend for themselves. From the ground we pulled a rope that released all the bars of their temporary home. At first they just stood there, wondering what to do next. Then…they flew off! It was so rewarding to see two eagles so tenderly and protectively cared for by their parents and then by the zoo staff finally set free to live the life they were designed and destined to live—
to discover their world and soar to amazing heights.

Let us guide our children with wisdom. Let us listen to their problems and help them find solutions. Let us give them unconditional love—no matter what. And when they are grown, let us find the courage to let go.

D. MORGAN

Lessons from the Wild

There are many things we can learn from a committed relationship—even if the relationship is between two birds. Our eaglets were blessed to have both parents available at all times to protect and educate them on how to become good, confident, adult eagles—to teach them to fly under the safety of their watchful eyes. They were also fortunate to have the opportunity to learn to adapt to their natural habitat. Though restricting and sometimes frustrating, the tower bars on the hacking tower were necessary protective boundaries for the young birds. They were removed only after the zoo staff determined that the eagles were ready for their new freedom and able to take care of themselves.

My wife, Suzi, and I have learned through raising our three beautiful and successful adult daughters that neither one of us could provide our children with the attention, opportunities, challenges, and boundaries they deserved without each other—but as a couple we could. We also learned that it was important to give our daughters "monitored freedom" and protective boundaries in order to help them adapt to the real world. As parents, our heart's desire is to teach, prepare, and surround our children with people, opportunities, and challenges that would help them become successful adults so they too can freely explore their world with confidence and make their dreams take flight.

*What greater thing is
there for human souls
than to feel that they are
joined for life—to be with
each other in silent
unspeakable memories.*
GEORGE ELIOT

Let's Stick Together
Zebras

My impression of life as a zebra is that everybody sticks together. Zebras are living examples of herd mentality. Herd living has many rewards, but in the end everyone is taking care of everyone else. And living together can be important for survival. For one thing, there are more eyes scanning the savannas for predators like lions.

While watching a herd of zebras in Kenya's Masai Mara reserve, I noticed that some zebras lowered their heads to graze as others watched for predators. All of a sudden, several lionesses appeared seemingly out of nowhere and began the chase—the race was on! One of the lions drew closer and closer to the thundering zebra herd, and then—just as suddenly as the chase began—she stopped. Dust filled the air as the lion watched its black-and-white prey gallop away. You see, when a lion begins to give chase, the zebra's herd behavior can help individuals escape by visually confusing their aggressor. For a lion to be successful in the hunt, it has to isolate a single individual. When zebras run away in a group, the lion sees a cluster of stripes, bodies, and hooves and must try to catch one of them, which is quite a challenge.

Zebra stripes are like human fingerprints in that no two zebra stripe patterns are exactly alike. Some zebras have wide, boldly colored stripes. Some zebras have small stripes of a lighter shade between their main stripes. Yet other zebras have thin pinstripes. So if you're a newborn zebra, how do you recognize your mother?

Successful imprinting is the answer. Just after a zebra is born, the mother makes sure her new baby knows who it is. Because the baby will follow anything that moves, the mother will keep all other zebras away from the foal, sometimes aggressively chasing away curious onlookers. This will go on for several days until the new baby recognizes its mom's odor and appearance.

The family.
We were a strange little band
of characters trudging through
life sharing diseases and
toothpaste, coveting one
another's desserts, hiding
shampoo, borrowing money,
locking each other out of our
rooms, inflicting pain and
kissing to heal it in the same
instant, loving, laughing,
defending, and trying to figure
out the common thread
that bound us all together.

ERMA BOMBECK

36

Lessons from the Wild

Zebras and other herd animals are perfect examples of strength in numbers. In a sense, they are like human families—they stick together through thick and thin. At least, that's how families should be. You grow up owing everything to your parents. They've protected and nurtured you, taught you, provided material things for you—and, I hope, have been there for emotional support whenever you needed it. As we love and respect our parents, our children will be watching and learning how to treat us. Likewise, nurturing lifelong bonds with our brothers and sisters will show our children how to do the same with one another.

To successfully imprint the value of sticking together as a family, we parents need to stick close to our own roots and family ties, support family members when they are weak, defend them when they are in danger, and actively love one another in good times and bad.

If you are blessed to still have your parents, call them and let them know how much you appreciate them. If you are blessed with siblings, call them and let them know how much you've enjoyed your friendship. Lastly, gather up your children and your spouse and let them know how much you treasure them and how blessed you are to have them in your family.

Gifts Come in
All Shapes and Sizes

Rhinos

I can still remember that scene in the old John Wayne movie *Hatari!* (a film about capturing animals for zoos). John Wayne's character was sitting in a chair on the hood of the capture truck as he and his team were racing across the African savanna trying to snare a black rhinoceros with a rope. The noose narrowly caught the rhino several times, which made the beast even more upset than he already was. All of a sudden, he charged the truck and slammed into it with a thunderous hit!

*Life began with waking up
and loving my mother's face.*
GEORGE ELIOT

Daniel Smith

Rhinos have always held a special place in my heart. Why? Maybe it is because of their prehistoric appearance, that unusual horn (which can grow to six feet in length), or just their nasty temperament. In fact, one of my most memorable wildlife experiences involves a baby rhino.

While in Zimbabwe, Africa, I was filming at a special place that cared for injured and orphaned animals of all kinds—the Chipangali Animal Orphanage, operated by Viv Wilson and his son, Kevin. When I first arrived they said they had a surprise for me—a newly born baby rhino! Only 19 days old, this little rhino calf was born to one of Chipangali's adult females and, unfortunately, his mother couldn't give him proper care.

Kevin led me to an indoor enclosure that was the baby's home. I stood there, just staring in awe at the odd-looking little rhino. He looked just like an adult, except that his "horn" was only a small bump near the end of his snout. His attendant was holding a large-scale baby bottle filled with milk high in the air as the rhino drank and drank and drank.

Then Kevin asked if I wanted to go inside with the baby—*Wow!*, I thought. I sat down in the straw and watched the funny antics of the infant beast. He was jumping, tossing his head around, and, of course, charging. He would charge at me with his head down and smack into me with his "horn" before twirling around and galloping away. After about 15 minutes of this, I realized why the Wilsons named the baby "Thunder." He was really playful and one of the most endearing baby animals I've ever had the pleasure of meeting.

The very aspect of the rhino that makes it so interesting has led to its demise. Rhino horn is highly prized in certain parts of the world for many reasons.

(By the way, a rhino's "horn" isn't a horn at all; it is actually tightly compressed keratin, a fingernail-like material.) Unfortunately, the rhino must be killed in order to harvest the valuable horn. This horn is a dilemma for rhinos. Without it, the rhino couldn't spar with others, nor have that majesty about its appearance. But with the horn, it is subject to being killed by poachers. Although rhinos are an endangered species and highly protected, the illegal killing of rhinos hasn't been stopped.

There comes that mysterious meeting in life
when someone acknowledges who we are
and what we can be, igniting the circuits
of our highest potential.
RUSTY BERKUS

Lessons from the Wild

It's amazing to me that the valuable protrusion from the snout of the rhino is what makes it

so unique and outstanding in the animal world, while at the same time, it has been the cause

of its endangerment. I can't help but think about the valuable little gifts and talents that we

notice in our children—the "little horns" that must be fostered and nurtured to grow into

characteristics that will make them stand out from the crowd. As parents, part of our

responsibility is to help our children identify their gifts and talents and then teach them to

treasure, grow, and guard those gifts and talents from forces and people (sometimes themselves)

who would rob them, or harm them, because of their uniqueness.

What "little horns" have you noticed in your children? If loved and protected, they will grow

into features that will give beauty and dignity to your children's lives.

Striped Tales
Tigers

Tigers are among the most striking creatures in the world, with wild black stripes adorning their bodies. What a sight for the early explorers who first spotted one! Of course, local people in the tiger's native lands had both feared and revered them for thousands of years. This great cat is a symbol of wildness and of power and is worthy of respect.

You never forget an encounter with a tiger. This cat is so formidable that nothing can escape its grasp. Yet this same animal is as gentle as a kitten when caring for its cubs.

Zoos and animal parks have been remarkably successful in breeding many animals, both endangered and common. Tigers, like most other cats, breed so well that their families have to be held in check. For the better part of the last half century, animal parks and zoos have supplied themselves with animals and have avoided taking creatures from the wild. In fact, most reputable zoos today raise funds for worldwide conservation, as they realize animals must be protected in their natural habitats.

Ika was a stunning white male tiger who called the Columbus Zoo home. The zoo was expecting the shipment of a new tiger, this one a common orange cat named Sheeba, any day.

When a new animal comes into the zoo, it is treated with kid gloves. There are stringent policies about the ways certain animals will be integrated into exhibits and with other animals. Everything starts with an "introduction," which can take many forms and be carried out over periods of weeks or months.

The strength
of motherhood
is greater
than natural laws.
BARBARA KINGSOLVER

Sheeba arrived in a large crate via an animal-transport van along with the Columbus zookeepers who cared for her on the journey from her former home, a circus. Now Sheeba would be able to enjoy her life after a career of performing—a kind of retirement.

The zookeepers carefully unloaded the crate and wheeled it past indoor animal enclosures filled with wild cats. When they approached Ika's area, they expected the usual—scowls, growls, and roars typical of two tigers meeting for the first time. Incredibly, what the keepers heard were "chuffing" sounds, basically a vocalization that tigers use as a friendly greeting. When Sheeba was transferred into her enclosure (next door to Ika's) she went directly to the steel door that separated the two and lay down (apparently, as close as she could get to Ika). Although she couldn't see him, Sheeba could obviously detect his odor. Tigers are normally solitary, preferring to avoid other tigers except for breeding situations. This was a little puzzling.

As the days passed, it was apparent that Sheeba and Ika could be introduced to each other in the same exhibit much sooner than expected. The steel door was slowly opened, and Sheeba walked directly through and toward Ika, where they met and nuzzled. After that, the two were inseparable. Even though they could have enjoyed a spacious outdoor exhibit, most of the time they stuck together. They sat together, lay down together, and always seemed to have contact with each other, even if it was only an outstretched paw touching the other cat.

Curiosity got the best of us, so we called Sheeba's previous owner and learned that the two cats actually knew each other from years and years ago when they performed in the circus together! After all that time, it only took a few seconds for the cats to recognize each other as old friends.

There may be less than 6000 tigers living in the wild. It is of utmost importance that each tigress raises her cubs properly so they can grow up and help in replenishing the dwindling population. It is equally important that their wild habitats be saved and poaching be stopped.

Three to six tiger cubs are born at a time, but usually only two or three survive. As with many animals, baby tigers are completely dependent upon their mothers for all their needs (until they are almost 15 months old and can begin to hunt on their own). Tigers are solitary creatures for the most part, but the father tiger sometimes plays a role in keeping other males away from mother and cubs because males have been known to kill newborns. As with giant pandas, it is the mother tiger that does all the rearing and teaching. After the first three to four months, the cubs begin following mom when she goes hunting. On these journeys through the forest, the little striped cats learn important hunting lessons about which animals to hunt and how to stalk them.

Lessons from the Wild

Tigers are powerful, yet they are the gentlest of creatures when rearing their cubs. We, too, have

to watch ourselves with our babies—although they are a bundle of joy and like to play, we have

to be careful to play gently.

And, just like tiger cubs, from the formative moments onward, our children

learn from their mothers and fathers. Teaching our youngsters the lessons of

life, along with emotional survival techniques they'll need as they grow, can be

both our greatest joy and greatest responsibility.

For the mother is and must be,
whether she knows it or not,
the greatest, strongest, and most
lasting teacher her children have.

HANNAH WHITALL SMITH

Hug Me Close
Koalas

Quietly creeping through the bush country—shhhhh—I saw a mob of kangaroos in the distance. They stopped foraging, looked up, and stared at me. I was surrounded by huge pine trees and unusual eucalyptus trees, very straight and towering above. All of a sudden, a monitor lizard (looking like a miniature dragon) scampered by!

We were filming *Animal Adventures* in the land down under—Australia. The scene was perfect and just as you'd imagine. The only thing missing were the haunting sounds of the didgeridoo (the long wooden flute of the Aborigines).

Australia is a land of very odd animals. Even some of their names are strange…dibbler, quoll, bandicoot. Most mammals there are marsupials (babies that are born at an immature stage and develop in the mother's pouch). Two exceptions are the extremely odd platypus and echidna (known as monotremes, or egg-laying mammals).

In the Pilliga Forest (some one million acres of vast wildlife habitat), I was accompanied by members of the Australian Koala Foundation (AKF) as we searched for one of the most endearing furry animals in the world—the koala. Not to be confused with a bear, a koala is a marsupial. This habitat wasn't the most comfortable place to be, with summertime temperatures reaching 130 degrees Fahrenheit, but the koalas seemed to like it. With their population now estimated to be less than 100,000 in the wild, koalas are closely watched by the AKF and other wildlife organizations.

We were lucky. After hiking for just about an hour, we found our quest—a female koala high atop a eucalyptus tree. I looked through the binoculars for a closer view and spied a surprise—a tiny baby clinging to her mother's back! We ended up with two for one and a perfect opportunity to examine how both koala mom and baby were faring.

The AKF had a professional tree-climber who scaled the tall tree and coaxed the koalas to the ground. I waited at the bottom with the veterinarians and other biologists who rescued them in a cloth bag and anesthetized them. The vets monitored all health conditions, weighed these adorable creatures, and were set to release them.

Still a little groggy from their "sleep," the koalas were taken back to their tree. Mom was placed at the base, and baby was carefully put on her back. As soon as the little one grasped tightly, the mother waddled up the tree, safe and sound.

My favorite place to be is
inside of your hugs
where it's warm and loving.
AUTHOR UNKNOWN

A hug is an amazing thing—it's the perfect way to show the love
we're feeling but can't find the words to say. It's funny how a little hug
makes everyone feel good; in every place and language,
it's always understood. And hugs don't need new equipment,
special batteries or parts. Just open up your arms
and open up your heart.

AUTHOR UNKNOWN

Lessons from the Wild

Mammal and bird babies are very delicate and defenseless, relying upon their mothers or parents for total care. But nothing compares with newborn marsupials.

When koalas are first born, they weigh less than one gram and are less than one inch long. A koala "joey" has no ears and is blind and totally hairless—that's what I call being a little helpless. Happily, though, mother koalas are built complete with pouches. The tiny baby—with its inborn sense of direction—makes its way from the birth canal into the pouch. Life in the pouch is great for a newborn koala, where it receives all the food and protection it could ever desire.

As baby koala grows, it eventually emerges from the pouch for a look outside. It spends more and more time out of the pouch and soon learns to ride on mom's back. Ahhh, but the pouch is still a wonderful thing. Anytime a young koala feels the urge, it simply climbs back in.

The attraction of a koala mother's pouch to a joey can be compared to a loving hug. Whenever you want to protect or be close to your children, give them a big hug—it's a marvelous feeling! Being hugged by a loved one is a reinforcement of affection and security for children—just like a koala baby climbing back into mom's pouch.